MIGUEL DE
CERVANTES

NOVELIST, POET, AND PLAYWRIGHT

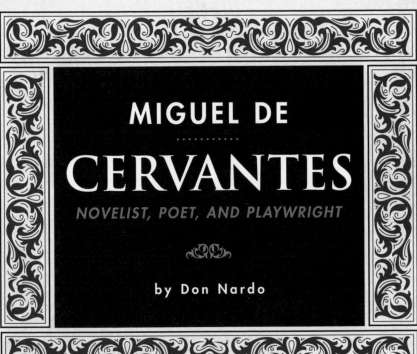

MIGUEL DE
CERVANTES
NOVELIST, POET, AND PLAYWRIGHT

by Don Nardo

(G)o

Content Adviser: Donna LeGrand, Ph.D.,
Associate Professor of Spanish,
Bethel University

Reading Adviser: Rosemary G. Palmer, Ph.D.,
Department of Literacy, College of Education,

Compass Point Books ⟡ Minneapolis, Minnesota

Compass Point Books
3109 West 50th Street, #115
Minneapolis, MN 55410

Copyright © 2008 by Compass Point Books
All rights reserved. No part of this book may be reproduced without written permission
from the publisher. The publisher takes no responsibility for the use of any of the
materials or methods described in this book, nor for the products thereof.
Printed in the United States of America.

This book was manufactured with paper containing at least
10 percent post-consumer waste.

Editor: Jennifer VanVoorst
Page Production: Ashlee Schultz
Photo Researcher: Svetlana Zhurkin
Cartographer: XNR Productions, Inc.
Library Consultant: Kathleen Baxter

Creative Director: Keith Griffin
Editorial Director: Nick Healy
Managing Editor: Catherine Neitge

Library of Congress Cataloging-in-Publication Data
Nardo, Don.
  Miguel de Cervantes : novelist, poet, and playwright / by Don Nardo.
      p. cm. — (Signature lives)
  Includes bibliographical references and index.
  ISBN 978-0-7565-3675-6 (library binding)
1. Cervantes Saavedra, Miguel de, 1547–1616. 2. Authors,
Spanish—Classical period, 1500–1700—Biography—Juvenile literature.
I. Title. II. Series.
  PQ6337.N25 2007
  863'.3—dc22
  [B]   2007035562

Visit Compass Point Books on the Internet at *www.compasspointbooks.com*
or e-mail your request to *custserv@compasspointbooks.com*

Signature Lives

RENAISSANCE ERA

The Renaissance was a cultural movement that started in Italy in the early 1300s. The word *renaissance* comes from a Latin word meaning "rebirth," and during this time, Europe experienced a rebirth of interest and achievement in the arts, science, and global exploration. People reacted against the religion-centered culture of the Middle Ages to find greater value in the human world. By the time the Renaissance came to a close, around 1600, people had come to look at their world in a brand new way.

Miguel de Cervantes

Table of Contents

1 BRAVERY AT LEPANTO

Chapter

⤳⥀⥀⤳

Twenty-four-year-old Miguel de Cervantes steadied himself by gripping a railing that ran along the side of the ship. The vessel—loaded with soldiers holding weapons—was on an attack run. It shook and heaved as it sped through the water. From his vantage point, the young man could see the enemy ships approaching fast. They filled his view from horizon to horizon. Their wooden decks were crowded with warriors whose single-minded aim, he knew, was to kill him and his companions. There is no way to know what Cervantes was thinking in the final seconds before the bloodbath began. But he may well have reflected one last time on how he had ended up in Greece on that fateful day in 1571.

A Spaniard, Cervantes had enlisted as a soldier

Miguel de Cervantes was among the soldiers in the Holy League who fought the Ottoman Turks in the naval battle at Lepanto, Greece, in 1571.

the year before. He became one of about 3,000 troops commanded by the distinguished Spanish officer Don Miguel de Moncada. Moncada's unit was stationed in Naples, a small city on Italy's western coast. At the time, Naples and its wide, picturesque bay belonged to Spain.

One of the reasons that Cervantes joined the service may have been his desire to fight the Turks. For some time, the Turkish Ottoman Empire, centered in the Middle East, had been threatening parts of Eastern Europe. The Turks were Muslims. In contrast, nearly all Europeans, including the Spanish, were Christians. European leaders, especially Pope Pius V, felt that the Turks threatened their faith and their way of life. Cervantes shared this view. He was eager to defend both his country and religion against what he saw as barbaric intruders.

This threat from the east became greater than ever in July 1570. The Turks invaded the large Mediterranean island of Cyprus. The pope responded by calling on all Christian states to unite. Many answered this call, which resulted in the formation of the Holy League early in 1571. Among its members were Spain, Venice, the Republic of Genoa (in Italy), and the Duchy of Savoy (in southeastern France).

The Holy League immediately assembled a large war fleet. It consisted of nearly 300 warships and more than 70,000 sailors and fighters. Commanding

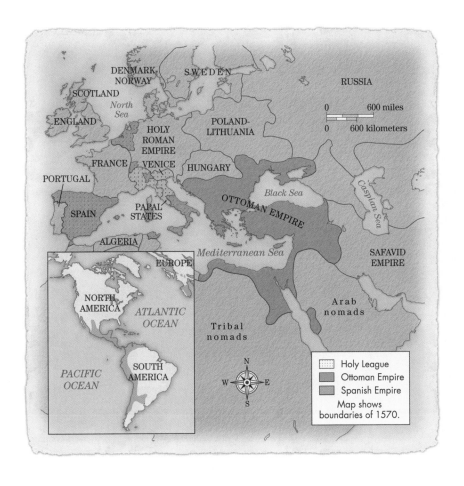

these forces was Austria's Don Juan, the half-brother of Spain's King Philip II. Don Juan had already gained a reputation as a war hero for destroying many Muslim pirate ships. In September 1571, he ordered the fleet to sail for Greece. There, he said, the fleet would halt the Turkish advance. Cervantes was assigned to a vessel named the *Marquesa*, captained by an Italian, Francisco de Santo Pietro.

The Turkish Ottoman Empire threatened the countries of the Holy League.

Don Juan of Austria (center), was assisted by Marc Antonio Colonna (left) and Sebastiano Venier in commanding the Holy League forces in the Battle of Lepanto.

Like many of the wooden European warships of that day, the *Marquesa* was powered by both sails and oars. It was roughly 130 feet (39 meters) long, but only about 16 feet (5 m) wide. That did not leave much room for the 200 rowers, 30 sailors, and 200 fighters it carried, plus their weapons and food. With so many men and supplies crammed into a very small space, such ships were cramped, filthy, and smelly. They were also infested with rats and bugs. These conditions appalled Cervantes. Seasick, suffocated, eaten by fleas and lice, and disgusted by the uncleanliness of himself and the crew, he was miserable during the weeks he spent on board before the battle.

Eventually, Cervantes' discomfort turned to illness. Not long before the allied fleet attacked the Turks near Lepanto, in western Greece, he came down with a high fever. Captain Santo Pietro told him he could rest belowdecks during the battle, but he refused. Grabbing his weapons and dragging himself on deck, he told Santo Pietro and the other ship's officers:

> *Gentlemen, on every occasion up to today in which His Majesty has been offered a fight into which I have been ordered, I have served well, as a good soldier; I shall do no less now, even though I am sick and feverish. Better that I fight in the service of God and His Majesty and die for them than to skulk [creep around] below deck.*

Bowing respectfully, he added: "Captain, put me in the most dangerous post there is—I will stick to it and die fighting!"

The captain was impressed by Cervantes' ardent sense of duty and agreed to let him fight. He even put the young man in charge of 12 soldiers charged with protecting one side of the ship. It was at this station that Cervantes found himself as the opposing fleets collided on October 7, 1571.

As the battle commenced, warships on both sides began ramming runs. These vessels had sturdy wooden or metal rams mounted on their prows, or front ends. The object was to speed toward, strike, and punch a hole in an enemy ship, causing it to sink. The fighters on both sides also unleashed deadly rains of lead balls shot from harquebuses. These were heavy, primitive guns that fired when the operator touched a flame to a pan of gunpowder. Also, some captains moved their ships alongside enemy vessels. Soldiers leaped from one vessel to another and fought hand to hand with swords and clubs.

The Holy League forces attacked Turkish ships with a variety of weapons and techniques.

As the battle raged, Cervantes repeatedly fired his harquebus. He also tried not to be overcome

by the huge assault of terrifying sights. Meanwhile, the sounds of shattering oars, blaring trumpets, gunshots, and raised human voices were almost deafening. One of the Italian soldiers present that day later wrote:

> The sound of the trumpets, … of drums became terrible, but still more so the noise of the harquebuses clacking, and the thunder of artillery. So piercing were the cries, so intense the clamor, … one was bewildered with terror. … The men are mad, they shout, howl, laugh, weep.

> The harquebus that Cervantes and other soldiers wielded at Lepanto was an early form of a hand-held gun. When the gunner pulled the trigger, a small flame ignited some gunpowder inside the gun, which fired off a lead ball. By about 1500, the harquebus was used by soldiers throughout Europe. It had two serious drawbacks, however. First, it took a long time to reload. Also, it was only accurate to 50 yards (45.5 meters).

In the midst of this chaos and butchery, Cervantes suddenly felt enemy gunshots jolt his body. Two lead balls entered his chest, and a third struck his hand. As he later described it: "By a deep hurt I felt my breast wounded, and the left hand was broken in a thousand pieces." Yet these severe wounds were not enough to stop the determined young man. To the amazement of his fellow soldiers, he summoned the strength to pull himself to his feet and resume fighting.

Don Juan, the commander of the Holy League's navy at Lepanto, was born in 1547. He was the son of King Carlos I of Spain and the half brother of King Philip II. In 1568, Don Juan defeated a number of Muslim pirates based in North Africa. Three years later, Philip made him commander of the Holy League's expedition to Greece. Don Juan's decisive victory at Lepanto made him a hero across Europe. English poet G.K. Chesterton later lavished praise on him in the poem "Lepanto." Don Juan died in 1578 during a military campaign in Belgium.

Eventually, it became clear to Cervantes and his companions that the Holy League had prevailed against the Turks. He later recalled the exciting moment of victory:

> The blood froze in their [the Turks'] veins when by the sound of our trumpets they learned of their loss and of our glory. The high victorious voice signaling, piercing the air, clear as day, showed that the Christian right had prevailed.

Cervantes emerged from the battle physically damaged but proud. His left hand had been badly mangled and could no longer be used. Thereafter, many people he knew affectionately called him "the handless one of Lepanto." He later wrote about his injury: "[H]owever unsightly it may appear, he looks upon [it] as beautiful, for the reason that it was received on the most memorable and sublime occasion that past ages have known."

Clearly, Cervantes believed strongly that people should fight for what they think is right. This

belief inspired his work first as a soldier and later as a writer. His experiences, too, found their way into his fiction. When he wrote his greatest novel, its leading character—the would-be knight Don Quixote—reflected both Cervantes' experiences and beliefs. Quixote was willing to give his life to uphold honor and justice, just as his creator had been in the bloody waters of Lepanto. ❧

Don Juan and his forces celebrated their victory over the Ottoman Turks.

2 A FAMILY ON THE MOVE

❧

The man who wrote one of the world's most beloved works of fiction—*Don Quixote*—was born in 1547 in Spain. The identity of Miguel de Cervantes' hometown is not in question. He came into the world in Alcalá de Henares, a town lying about 20 miles (32 kilometers) northeast of Madrid, in central Spain.

However, the exact date of his birth remains uncertain. But Miguel's certificate of baptism has survived. It is dated October 9, 1547. It was then the custom to baptize babies as soon after their births as possible. This was because the rate of infant mortality was high. Many newborns perished before they were a year old. Spaniards were devout Catholics. They wanted to make sure these unfortunate children were baptized before they died to ensure their entrance

The Port of Seville, painted in the 16th century by Alonzo Sanchez Coello

into heaven. Based on these facts, modern scholars estimate that Miguel was born on September 29 or perhaps a day or two later.

Very little is known about Miguel de Cervantes' childhood, including his family life and education. His later biographers pieced together what is known mostly by examining public documents that mention him and his relatives. There are also a few short passages in his adult writings that seem to describe situations from his youth.

Cervantes' baptism certificate, issued by the Church of Saint Mary the Great in Alcalá de Henares, reads: "Sunday nine days of the month of October in the Year of our Lord one thousand and five and forty and seven years was baptized Miguel, son of Rodrigo de Cervantes and his wife Doña Leonor, his godfather Juan Pardo, and he who baptized him, the Reverend Serrano, priest of Our Lady, attested by ... I who baptized him and sign my name."

Of the public documents, the boy's baptism certificate is an example. It states his parents' names: Rodrigo de Cervantes and Doña Leonor de Cortinas. Other surviving evidence indicates that Rodrigo made his living as a surgeon. That term did not have the same meaning it does now— a skilled doctor who performs operations. In medieval Spain, a surgeon was actually a sort of doctor's assistant. Such an assistant was allowed to set broken bones and perform other minor medical procedures. However, he lacked the skills and social standing of a full-fledged physician.

A surgeon was able to perform minor medical procedures, such as stitching up a wounded leg.

A surgeon also made a good deal less money than a doctor, so the Cervantes family was never very well off. Indeed, they often had difficulty making ends meet. This may have annoyed Rodrigo's wife, Doña Leonor. In a one-act play Cervantes wrote many years later, *The Divorce Court Judge*, one of the characters is a surgeon's wife. The complaint she voices in the following passage may be loosely based on words he once heard his mother say:

*I was fooled when I married him because
he told me he was a genuine, pulse-taking
physician and he turned out to be a surgeon, a man who fixes splints and cures
minor ailments, which makes him worth
half a doctor in value.*

Despite his modest income and social position,
Rodrigo was a proud and ambitious man. Whenever
possible, he presented himself as a *hidalgo*. The
members of the hidalgo class claimed descent from
Spain's noblest families. If they had the proper
documents to prove it, they received certain special
privileges. They were exempt from paying taxes,
for example. Also, they could not be sent to prison
when they were unable to pay their debts, a common
custom at the time. Rodrigo did not have the papers
to prove he was a hidalgo. This sometimes got him
into trouble when the authorities asked to see them.

Rodrigo's efforts to improve his situation were
partly based on his desire to take advantage of his
country's great success. At the time, Spain was
a world power. The Spanish king, Carlos I, also
enjoyed the title Emperor Charles V. In addition to
Spain, his vast realm included the Mediterranean
islands of Sardinia and Sicily, parts of North Africa,
and large portions of the recently claimed Americas.
Charles was also heir to parts of Germany, Austria,
and the Netherlands. This mighty empire produced

immense wealth, in which Rodrigo de Cervantes hoped to share.

Unlike Miguel's father, his mother, Doña Leonor, did not feel comfortable talking about her ancestry. Her grandparents or great-grandparents had been *conversos*, Jews who had converted to Catholicism. Jews had long been hated and discriminated against in Spain. To escape such treatment, many had converted. Suspicions lingered, however, that some conversos were really *marranos*, false Christians who continued to practice Jewish rituals in secret. Thousands of suspected marranos were murdered shortly before Doña Leonor was born. She was a

A Jewish girl is accused of witchcraft.

sincere and devout Catholic. But she likely lived always with at least some fear of arrest.

Doña Leonor also imparted her Catholic beliefs to her children. Miguel was the fourth of her and Rodrigo's seven offspring. The first, a boy named Andres, had been born in 1543 but had died in infancy. Then came two girls—Andrea (1544) and Luisa (1546). After Miguel came another boy, named Rodrigo (1550) after his father. Still later came Magdalena (1552) and, finally, Juan (1554).

Rodrigo, Doña Leonor, and their first four surviving children at first dwelled in a small house with few comforts in Alcalá de Henares. But in 1551, hoping to improve their situation, Rodrigo moved the family to Valladolid. Lying about 125 miles (200 km) northwest of Madrid, Valladolid was one of Spain's most prosperous towns. However, Rodrigo's dreams of achieving success there came to nothing. Unable to pay his mounting debts, he spent several months in debtor's prison.

When the elder Cervantes was released in 1553, he moved his family back to Alcalá. It may have been then, when Miguel was 6, that he learned to read. There is no evidence that he entered a formal school at this time, and most scholars think that a distant relative, Alonso de Vieras, taught him the basics of reading and writing. At the time, Alcalá was a busy university town. In addition, a number of book

*Cervantes'
birthplace
in Alcalá de
Henares is now
a museum.*

publishers were located there, along with several bookshops. These may have been young Miguel's earliest exposure to the literary world.

It is unclear how long the boy remained in his hometown. Some evidence suggests that the following year, 1554, he went with his parents for an extended stay in Córdoba, in southern Spain. There, Miguel may have attended a Jesuit school. The Jesuits were and remain an order of Catholic priests renowned for their dedication to learning and teaching.

A Jesuit school did open in Córdoba in 1555, when Miguel was 8 years old. No definite proof exists that he was enrolled there. However, something he wrote later demonstrates an inside knowledge of how religious fathers, or priests, instructed young boys in such schools. He wrote in his novel *The Dialogue of the Dogs:*

> *I was pleased to see the love … and industry with which those blessed fathers and masters taught those boys. … I observed how gently they scolded them, how mercifully they punished them, how they inspired them with examples, gave them prizes as incentives, and how prudently they indulged them.*

The stay in Córdoba did not mark the end of the Cervantes family's travels. In 1564, when Miguel was 17 or 18, Rodrigo moved them to Seville, an important city situated southwest of Córdoba. There, the young man may have briefly attended the local Jesuit school. If he did study there, a kindly uncle likely paid the tuition, since Rodrigo lacked the funds.

The last family move that affected Miguel took place two years later. This time, he and the others settled in Madrid, which had recently become Spain's new capital. Firm evidence shows that the young man attended a local school. Its headmaster, Juan López de Hoyos, was impressed by Miguel's intelligence, diligence as a student, and flair for writing. The two became close friends. Hoyos left behind a note calling the young man "our dear and beloved disciple."

In 1568, Hoyos gave Miguel a special assignment. Elisabeth of Valois, wife of Spain's King Philip II, had just died at the age of 23. The headmaster asked the young man to compose four elegies, poems or songs of mourning, for the dead queen. The first poem began: "To whom will my sad song go? In whose ear will its voice resound that will not melt the heart to tears?" The beauty of these words demonstrates that Hoyos had chosen the right person to write the elegies. What the teacher could not foresee was that his star pupil was destined to become Spain's greatest writer. ✑

Elisabeth of Valois, Queen of Spain (1545–1568)

3 THE LIFE OF A SOLDIER

ⷮⵦⵯⵕ

About three years passed between the writing of the elegies for the dead queen and Miguel de Cervantes' participation in the battle of Lepanto. The events of his life in these years are sketchy at best. Evidence does show that he traveled from Spain to Italy. However, scholars still debate his motivation for leaving his native country.

Within a year of leaving Spain, Cervantes joined the military. However, the reasons he did so are also uncertain. Following the fight at Lepanto, where he was wounded, he remained in the service for four more years. During that period he saw more action. Regrettably, though, the exact details of these exploits have not survived. It is possible to piece together only a bare outline of Cervantes' life between 1569 and

Miguel de Cervantes was among the soldiers who captured the city of Tunis in 1573.

1575. However, his major movements can be traced with reasonable surety.

For example, there is no doubt that Cervantes was settled in Rome by December 1569. He was now 22 years old. It is also certain that he was now employed in a minor capacity in the Vatican. This was—and still is—the sector of Rome in which the pope and other high Catholic officials lived and worked.

What modern scholars cannot agree on is why the young man left Spain and how he acquired the Vatican job. One theory is that while living in Madrid, Cervantes got into an argument and fought a duel. The fight took place near King Philip's palace. Dueling so near the royal residence was a crime punishable by cutting off the offender's right hand. So, the story goes, Cervantes fled the country. Part of the evidence cited for this scenario consists of passages from his later writings. These involve Spanish characters who fight duels and then flee to Italy. Some experts think these fictional incidents are based on Cervantes' real experiences.

Other scholars disagree, however. They think that these fictional passages are just that—fictional. It is more likely, they say, that Cervantes left Spain because he had already been hired for the Vatican job. Late in 1568, Pope Pius V sent a papal diplomat, Monsignor Julio Acquaviva, to Madrid. Acquaviva met with King Philip on a variety of matters. This theory suggests that during these meetings the Italian read the elegies Cervantes had written for the recently deceased queen. Acquaviva was greatly impressed. According to biographer Francisco Ledesma:

> *Acquaviva promised to take such a mature talent with him to Italy. He already had Italian poets in his service and to the monsignor it seemed no bad thing to add to their company a Spanish chamberlain [youth] who could versify [compose verses] so sweetly.*

The Vatican is dominated by St. Peter's Basilica, as seen across the Tiber River and St. Angelo's Bridge.

In whatever manner Cervantes ended up in Rome, he served with Acquaviva for a little less than a year. The young man's exact position is unknown. He may have been the monsignor's secretary, or he might have been his butler or a manservant in charge of his clothes and personal items.

No matter the job, it is likely that Cervantes felt fortunate to have it. After all, he was living and working in Rome. Not only was that city crammed with history and culture, it lay at the very heart of the Christian world and faith. This was both educational and exciting for a young Catholic who had never before ventured outside his native country. Cervantes later expressed his fascination and passion for Rome through a character who visits the city in his short novel *The Glass Licentiate:*

What did Cervantes look like as an adult? He described himself in one of his later works: "The man you see here with the ... chestnut hair, the smooth, untroubled brow, the bright eyes, the hooked yet well-proportioned nose, the silvery beard that less than a score of years ago was golden, the big mustache, ... the body of medium height, ... the high complexion that is fair rather than dark, the slightly stooping shoulders and the somewhat heavy build—this, I may tell you, is the author [who is] commonly called Miguel de Cervantes."

> *He visited its temples, worshiped its saintly relics, and admired its grandeur. ... Rome is revealed by its broken marbles, whole and half statues, broken arches and ruined baths ... by its bridges which*

seem to mirror each other, and by its streets whose names alone claim authority over those of all the other cities of the world. ... He also noted the authority of the College of Cardinals, the dignity of the Supreme Pontiff [the pope], the crowds of varied people and nations.

At some point in 1570, Cervantes and Acquaviva parted company. This may have been because the monsignor was promoted to the post of cardinal and no longer needed the young man's services. Or perhaps Cervantes decided for reasons of his own to

A 16th-century illustration of the Audience Chapel at the Vatican

quit his position at the Vatican.

What is certain is that by the fall of that same year the young Spaniard had enlisted in the military. Some modern scholars and other observers find this move puzzling. Why, they ask, did Cervantes choose to be a soldier rather than a writer at this crucial point in his life? As scholar Arnoldo Mondadori suggests, the patriotic young man may have felt "impelled by the religious zeal then sweeping Europe for a new campaign against the hated Moslem Turks."

When he joined the Spanish military, Cervantes was assigned to Don Miguel de Moncada's forces, stationed in Naples. The young man immediately got along with his captain, Don Diego de Urbina. This was likely in part because they had been neighbors in Spain. Don Diego hailed from a town very near Cervantes' hometown of Alcalá de Henares.

Cervantes found that soldiering had both drawbacks and benefits. He later listed some of the bad points of military life in his masterpiece, *Don Quixote:*

> *There is no one poorer [than a soldier], for he is dependent on his miserable pay, which comes late or never, ... and in the depth of winter he has to defend himself against the ... weather ... with nothing better than the breath of his mouth. ... Then, after all this, suppose the day ... of battle to have arrived ... [and] left him*

Ceramic tiles from the 1570s of Spanish soldiers

with a crippled arm or leg. Or if this does not happen, and merciful Heaven watches over him and keeps him safe and sound, it may be he will be in the same poverty he was in before.

On the other hand, Cervantes saw certain advantages in soldiering. These included defending his country and religion, making new friends, and gaining a reputation as a brave and honorable man. He later wrote of his military days:

> *I acquired the name of a good soldier.*
> *The emperor distinguished me, I made*
> *friends, and above all, I learned liberality*
> *and good breeding—one learns this in the*
> *school of a Christian soldier.*

Miguel de Cervantes (1547–1616)

Cervantes was certainly proud of his service at Lepanto, where the Christian fleet defeated the Turks in October 1571. The severe wounds he received in the battle required that he spend six months in a hospital. After his release in April 1572, he returned to the Spanish base at Naples. There, he spent some time with his younger brother Rodrigo, who had also fought at Lepanto.

The following year, Miguel de Cervantes served again under the victor of Lepanto, Don Juan of Austria. In October 1573, Don Juan's forces attacked

North Africa. Cervantes, now 26, was among the soldiers who captured the town of Tunis, long a stronghold of Muslim pirates. He had no way of knowing at the time that this would not be his last trip to Africa. Soon he would return, not as a soldier but as a prisoner. ℘

The Battle of Lepanto prevented the Turks from expanding their empire into Europe.

Chapter

4 FIVE YEARS IN A DUNGEON

ɷໜɷ

In 1575, after nearly five years of service in the military, Miguel de Cervantes had every intention of remaining a soldier. He planned to return to Spain and there be promoted to the rank of captain, so he obtained some letters of recommendation from high-ranking Spanish officers. One came from the famous Don Juan himself. With high hopes, in September 1575 Cervantes and his brother Rodrigo boarded the *El Sol*, a ship bound for Spain.

But the two did not make it to their homeland. On September 26, 1575, a squadron of Turkish ships appeared seemingly out of nowhere and attacked. Many people on board the *El Sol* were killed. The Cervantes brothers were captured and bound in chains. They soon found themselves in Algiers, on the coast of North Africa. A bustling Muslim city of 150,000 people, Algiers was one of the leading trading centers of the Mediterranean world. It was also a major slave market. Its prisons held 25,000 Christian captives.

Cervantes hoped for a quick release, but it was not to be. To his horror and regret, he remained a captive for five long years. His stay in Algiers was so miserable and frightening that it colored his thinking for the rest of his days. As scholar Maria Garcés points out:

A 17th-century engraving of the slave market in Algiers

The story of his traumatic experience continuously speaks through Cervantes's fictions. His [works are] haunted by images of captivity: cages of all sizes, Christian captives, galley slaves, and female prisoners. … One wonders whether Cervantes could have become the great creative writer that he was had he not suffered the traumatic experience of his Algerian captivity.

Cervantes, now 28, was a highly observant and quick-witted individual, so it did not take him long to size up the situation and see where he fit within it. He noted that the Christian captives were divided into two groups. The less fortunate prisoners were those who had no well-to-do relatives or friends in their home countries. Unable to collect ransoms for these captives, the Turks made them slaves. As slaves, they had to do backbreaking work in the streets, on ships, and in Muslim homes. They were also brutalized and killed on a regular basis. Cervantes later described the cruelties his master inflicted upon the Christians:

Images of captivity and the horrors of prison life abound in Cervantes' literary works. However, none of his works contains more direct references to his five-year imprisonment in Algiers than his play Life in Algiers. He wrote it in the early 1580s, shortly after his return to Spain. Its tone is partly comical and partly serious, and it contains mostly fictional characters. However, many of the situations it describes are likely ones that Cervantes witnessed or experienced when he was a captive in Algiers.

Every day he hanged a man, impaled one, cut off the ears of another; and all with so little provocation … that the Turks acknowledged he did it merely for the sake of doing it.

Cervantes and his brother counted themselves lucky to be in the second group of prisoners. They were the ones who might fetch large ransoms to fill their captors' pockets. A Turk named Dali Mami found Cervantes' letters of recommendation from Don Juan and other Spanish officers. The letters convinced Mami that the Cervantes brothers came from a wealthy family and would bring in a lot of cash. It was in the Turks' interests to keep the two men in reasonably good shape. Cervantes later wrote:

[W]hen it was discovered that I was a captain, nothing could dissuade them from including me among the gentlemen and those waiting to be ransomed. They put a chain on me … and so I passed my life in that prison with several other gentlemen and persons of quality marked out as held to ransom.

Though Cervantes and the others awaiting ransom were not maimed or killed, their lives were still miserable. In addition to wearing chains, they had to perform tiring chores. Cervantes himself was forced to carry heavy bundles of supplies through the streets. His crippled left hand made this particularly difficult. In addition, Muslim bystanders spit on or threw rocks at him as he shuffled along.

Cervantes did what he had to in order to survive his awful predicament. However, he was not very hopeful about being ransomed. What Mami and the other Turks did not know was that the Cervantes family was far from rich. Miguel and Rodrigo's parents still lived on the verge of poverty. There was no way they could afford to pay the huge ransoms.

A map of Algiers from the 1572 Civitates Orbis Terrarum by Georg Braun and Frans Hogenberg

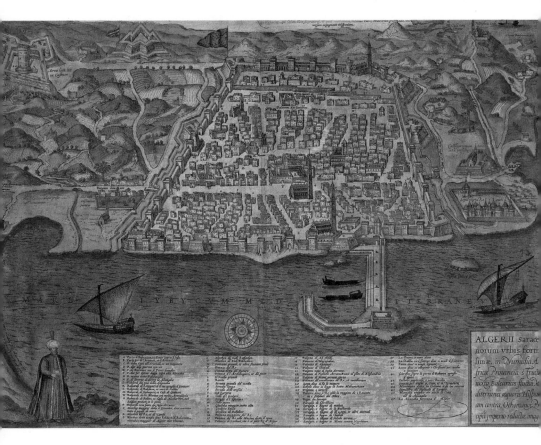

The Turks had demanded 500 ducats, equal to hundreds of thousands of today's dollars, for Miguel's release alone.

Therefore, Cervantes reasoned, he had only one realistic option: escape. His first daring attempt to gain freedom occurred early in 1576. He persuaded a local Muslim to guide him and some other prisoners to Oran. That Spanish-held North African city was separated from Algiers by 220 miles (352 km) of desert. Unfortunately for the escapees, their guide abandoned them soon after they entered the desert. They had no idea of where to look for water and food in the scorching wilderness. The sufferings of a character in Cervantes' later work, *Life in Algiers*, likely mirror those he had himself experienced:

> *Now hunger afflicts me and insufferable thirst torments me; already my strength is waning; I hope to escape from this ordeal by giving myself up to whomever may want to recapture me.*

Sure enough, Cervantes and his companions were recaptured. The Turks did not punish him severely but instead put him under tighter guard. This is probably because they were still convinced he could be traded for a hefty ransom.

Undaunted, Cervantes refused to give up and spend the rest of his life as a prisoner. Not long after returning to captivity in Algiers, he began plotting another escape attempt. He did not yet know that this plan would be shaped in part by events then happening in Spain.

As expected, Miguel and Rodrigo's father was unable to raise any money for their ransoms. However, their mother, Doña Leonor, did manage to borrow 60 ducats. She gave the money to an order of Spanish monks. The monks regularly raised money from a variety of sources and used it to ransom Christian captives from the Turks. The monks secured Rodrigo's release in August 1577 by paying

Today Algiers is the capital city of Algeria.

300 ducats. They could not afford another 500 ducats for Miguel, however, so he remained in prison.

Now that Rodrigo was free, he tried to help his brother escape. Miguel de Cervantes had devised the scheme shortly before Rodrigo's release. The younger man hired a small ship. On a dark night in late September 1577, the vessel approached a beach near Algiers. There, the older Cervantes was waiting with 14 other Christian captives. But the plan failed when the sailors manning the ship lost their nerve and sailed away. Once more, Cervantes was recaptured and placed in chains.

The stubborn and fearless Spaniard still refused to give up. He planned and executed two more escape attempts, one in 1578 and the other in the following year. Both attempts also ended in failure.

But all was not lost for Cervantes. In 1580, another order of Christian monks began negotiating with the Algerian Turks for the release of specific prisoners. He was among these captives. In September of that year, a monk named Juan Gil secured his release. Free at last, 33-year-old

Cervantes' fourth and final escape attempt involved another Spaniard he met while in captivity. This man, Licentiate Giron, had recently converted to Islam, so he was a free citizen of Algiers. Cervantes convinced Giron to arrange for a ship to carry 60 prisoners to freedom. Giron borrowed the money to buy the ship. The prisoners promised to pool their resources later and pay him back. At the last minute, however, someone told the authorities what was happening, and the scheme fell apart.

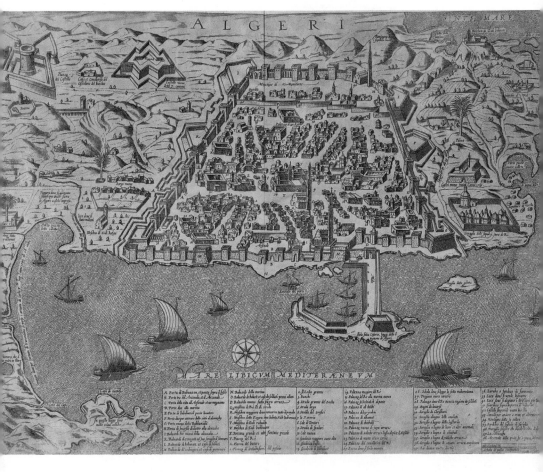

A 1572 engraving of Algiers

Miguel de Cervantes sailed for his native land, where his overjoyed family awaited. He had seen neither Spain nor his relatives (except for Rodrigo) for 10 long years.

47

5 NOVELIST, PLAYWRIGHT, AND HUSBAND

Chapter

⤷⤶

Miguel de Cervantes' captivity in Algiers between 1575 and 1580 had been the most miserable period of his life. In contrast, the five years that followed would turn out to be, overall, his happiest period. During these busy and eventful years he struggled to create a new life for himself. Financially broke, he searched desperately for decent-paying work. Finally, he decided to try to exploit a talent he had displayed in his youth—writing. Cervantes found that he greatly enjoyed both the writing process and socializing with writers, actors, and other artists. He also fell in love with two women during this period, and he married one of them. In addition, he spent time with his parents and siblings, whom he had not seen in many years.

Indeed, Cervantes had sorely missed his relatives. The family reunion that took place on his return to Spain late in 1580 was a joyful occasion for all. But Cervantes feared he might become a burden to his parents. He lacked both money and a decent job. His parents, too, were practically penniless.

Hoping to help both himself and his family, the young man tried to collect a pension, money awarded by the government for his military service. He composed a formal letter and sent it to the proper officials. To his dismay, he was turned down. There were simply too many former soldiers who were asking for pensions. The government could not afford to help them all.

The persistent Cervantes next tried asking the government for a job. He journeyed to the Spanish royal court. King Philip had just moved his government from Madrid to Lisbon, in nearby Portugal, which had recently become part of Spain's empire. At first, Philip's officials informed Cervantes that they had no work for him. However, in May 1581, he landed a temporary position as a royal messenger. His assignment was to deliver some important letters from King Philip to the Spanish governor of Oran, in North Africa. On his return to Spain, Cervantes asked the government to give him a post in the Americas. He was told that no jobs were presently available.

During the long months he was looking for work,

Cervantes had a lot of spare time on his hands. He needed something to fill his idle hours, and it made sense to choose a project that might eventually turn a profit. He fondly remembered the poetry he had written in his school days, and he recalled how impressed people had been with his writing talents. Reasoning that he could potentially make a living as a writer, he began working on a novel.

King Philip II of Spain (1527–1598)

Cervantes' chief concern was that the book would sell, so he decided to play it safe. Rather than try for originality, he chose a style that was already widely popular—the pastoral novel (or pastoral romance). Books in this style dealt mainly with country life. Typical characters included shepherds, milkmaids, and woodland spirits who had love affairs, weddings, duels, and various adventures.

Titled *La Galatea*, Cervantes' novel features two male friends—Elicio and Erastro. Both are in love with a beautiful shepherdess named Galatea. Erastro tells Elicio:

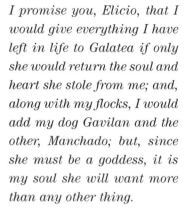

In writing his first novel, La Galatea, Cervantes copied the style of the Portuguese novelist and poet Jorge de Montemayor (c. 1520–1561). In particular, Cervantes was influenced by Montemayor's book Diana. Published in about 1559, it was the first pastoral novel written in Spanish. It set a trend later followed by many other writers, including Cervantes.

I promise you, Elicio, that I would give everything I have left in life to Galatea if only she would return the soul and heart she stole from me; and, along with my flocks, I would add my dog Gavilan and the other, Manchado; but, since she must be a goddess, it is my soul she will want more than any other thing.

Elicio, Erastro, Galatea, and Galatea's friend, Florisa, go on a journey to attend a wedding. They meet several characters along the way who tell colorful stories about themselves.

Cervantes completed the novel in 1583. In June 1584, he sold it to a book dealer, Blas de Robles, for 120 ducats. It was published the following year. Because of the author's strong writing skills, the book was well received. The noted Spanish playwright and poet Lope de Vega remarked, "[I]f it is a good book you want, you cannot ask for better."

Immediately after finishing *La Galatea*, Cervantes began writing plays. Evidence suggests that he turned out between 20 and 30 of them in the following four years. All but two of these works are now lost.

GALATEA
DIVIDIDA EN
SEYS LIBROS.

Compuesta por Miguel de Cervantes.

Dirigida al Illustrissimo Señor
Ascanio Colona Abad de
Sancta Sofia.

EN PARIS,
Por Gilles Robinot, en la calle de la Draperia a la
enseña del plato de estaño, y en la pequeña
galeria del Palacio.
M D C XI.
Con privilegio de su Magestad Christianissima.

*The title page
of Cervantes'
first novel,*
La Galatea

One of the lost plays, *The Naval Battle*, told the
story of the great conflict at Lepanto, in which the
author had fought. Another play that did not survive,

The Perplexed Lady, was Cervantes' favorite. "[I]f I do say so," he later wrote, it "can be singled out as good among the best of all the cloak-and-dagger dramas presented up to now."

Of the two plays that survived, the first written was *Life in Algiers.* Its characters are fictional, but it contains realistic descriptions of the horrors Cervantes experienced during his five-year captivity. The other surviving play is *Numantia,* or *The Siege of Numantia.* It dramatizes a Roman army's attack on the ancient Spanish town of Numantia.

While Cervantes was writing his first play, he sometimes visited a Madrid tavern where playwrights and actors hung out. There, he fell in love with the tavern owner's wife, Ana Franca de Rojas. Cervantes and the young woman produced a child out of wedlock—Isabel. Cervantes may not have known about the birth of Isabel, who spent most of her childhood believing her father was Ana's husband, Alonso Rodriguez.

Cervantes left Madrid in September 1584. He traveled to the village of Esquivias, situated several miles south of Madrid. There, he offered to help the family of one of his poet friends who had recently died. While in Esquivias, Cervantes met a beautiful young woman named Doña Catalina de Salazar. They fell in love and were married on December 12, 1584. At the time, he was 37, and she was 19.

Early in 1585, Cervantes and his bride moved into a comfortable two-story house in Esquivias. Cervantes was happy living with Doña Catalina. He also enjoyed taking short trips to Madrid to socialize with his writer and actor friends and to see his parents and sisters.

Cervantes' father died in June 1585, and the event changed the son's life. Cervantes now felt obliged to care for his widowed mother and unmarried sisters. This meant that he now had two families to support. His plays had made very little money. He had to face the reality that he could not make ends meet as a writer. Once more, with great reluctance, Miguel de Cervantes began looking for gainful employment.

The village of Esquivias, in which Cervantes met and wed his wife, lies in the charming region of La Mancha. It features lovely rolling hills, broad wheat fields, and lush vineyards. In Cervantes' time, there were also numerous windmills, which powered machinery that turned large millstones. The stones crushed wheat into flour used to make bread and pastries. Cervantes immediately fell in love with the area and later used it as the setting for the story he told in his masterpiece, Don Quixote.

6 An Unrewarding Career

Chapter

❧

Sometime in 1586, Miguel de Cervantes carefully examined his personal situation. His father had died the year before. By custom, when a father died, his sons assumed financial responsibility for their mother and any unmarried sisters. Cervantes had two brothers—Rodrigo and Juan—who might have shared in the obligation. But Rodrigo had re-entered the military, and for reasons that are now unclear, Juan was unable to help.

That left Cervantes to support his mother and sisters in Madrid. He also needed to support his wife in Esquivias. These burdens proved to be too much for an aspiring writer to bear, as scholar Arnoldo Mondadori explains:

King Philip II assembled the huge fleet known as the Spanish Armada to invade England.

With the sudden doubling of his family responsibilities, he [Cervantes] could no longer devote his energies to writing plays and novels without the certainty of immediate success and money to pay his heavy load of bills. With patience and time he had hoped to become famous and earn enough ... to keep his enlarged household going, but patience and hopes were not

Though he traveled widely as a soldier, Cervantes spent most of his life in Spain.

enough to feed and clothe his wife, his mother, and two sisters. What he needed immediately was a secure employment, and one for which he could expect to be well paid.

While Cervantes was looking for work, larger events were unfolding that directly affected his job prospects. Relations between Spain and England became increasingly strained, and early in 1587, a squadron of English ships, commanded by Sir Francis Drake, attacked a Spanish port town. The raiders destroyed more than 20 Spanish vessels. They also made off with the valuable cargoes these ships had been carrying.

Enraged, King Philip decided to retaliate by invading England. He began assembling a huge fleet of ships, which became known as the Spanish Armada. The fleet required enormous amounts of food and other provisions, so the government hired private contractors to collect the supplies. Cervantes managed to land one of these jobs and was assigned to the region of southern Spain.

Cervantes soon learned that

The Spanish originally called the Armada the "Great and Most Fortunate Navy." It consisted of about 130 ships of various sizes. They were outfitted with 1,500 brass cannons and 1,000 iron cannons, and they were manned by 8,000 sailors and 18,000 soldiers. The fleet was commanded by Don Alonso Pérez de Guzmán el Bueno, the seventh Duke of Medina Sidonia.

the task of acquiring the supplies was both difficult and frustrating. First, it involved many steps and responsibilities. He had to wander around the countryside and locate farms that produced large amounts of wheat, barley, corn, livestock, olive oil, and other essential items. He was also expected to store the goods and keep them safe from thieves. In addition, he had to ship the supplies to the fleet. All these steps required keeping accurate records of the amounts of food collected and shipped. Any mistakes would be costly for the government. Cervantes might lose his job or even go to jail. Unfortunately for him, he had a poor head for numbers, which increased the chances of his failing in the job.

Another frustrating part of the job was negotiating with farmers and landowners over the goods. Some demanded prices Cervantes could not meet. Others did not want to sell their products to the government at all. This is what happened when he arrived in the village of Écija. The government had bought wheat from its citizens before. These people had still not received their payments, however, so they refused to make any new deals with Cervantes.

The problem was that the navy badly needed the crops. Cervantes' boss ordered him to take the crops whether the villagers liked it or not. Very reluctantly, Cervantes began doing what he was told. However, some of the grain he collected belonged

Mowing Wheat, *from a 16th-century Flemish prayer book*

to the Catholic church in nearby Seville. Angry, the principal priest excommunicated him, or barred him from taking part in Catholic rituals. Because Cervantes was devoutly religious, he became extremely distressed at this turn of events.

Fortunately, Cervantes' boss journeyed to Écija and worked out a compromise with the villagers, and the church in Seville lifted the excommunication. However, Cervantes later ran into trouble with a church official in another town and was once again excommunicated.

The job had other disadvantages as well. The government was often late in paying Cervantes. This forced him to borrow money just to eat. Also, he had to spend long periods in the south, away from his wife, who still kept up the house in Esquivias. For these and other reasons, over time he came to hate the job.

In fact, the only good aspect of the job for Cervantes was the knowledge that he was helping the Spanish troops. Like other Spaniards, he was always eager to hear reports of the Armada's progress. He was thrilled when in the summer of 1588 news came that the fleet had been successful and the invasion of England was taking place. To celebrate the occasion, Cervantes happily composed some verses:

> [S]ing the valor of the sons of Spain, with which you glorify Heaven and terrify the earth. Tell ... how bodies flew through the air propelled by the fiery engines of war; how the waters changed their color and the blood of fearless hearts soaked the enemy soil; how this ship or another fled or fought fiercely.

It soon became clear, however, that the rosy reports of victory had been premature and false. In reality, the Armada had suffered a resounding defeat. The English had attacked the Spanish ships in the English Channel, forcing them to retreat. Then storms and other mishaps had taken a heavy toll. Altogether, more than 50 of the vessels, along with thousands of men, had been lost.

This distressing news prompted Cervantes to compose a second poem about the Armada. This time, he mourned the tragic losses. But he made

The defeat of the Spanish Armada led to the decline of Spanish power in the world.

it clear that the soldiers were not to blame for the disaster. Instead, he said, it was God's will. "[T]here is no apology for what heaven ordains," he wrote. Cervantes may have wondered if God would grant a Spanish victory later, for King Philip had already begun planning a second invasion.

A portrait of Cervantes was painted by Juan de Jauregui y Aguilar after the author's death.

Not long after the Spanish defeat, Cervantes received more bad news, this time of a more personal nature. Hoping to find a less stressful, more rewarding job, he had once more applied for a position in Spain's American colonies. Again he was rejected. This may have been partly because of his age. Cervantes was now in his 40s, and most of the men chosen for assignments in the Americas were in their 20s or 30s. His handicapped left hand may also have been a factor.

Even more upsetting for Cervantes were the corruption charges made against him in 1592. People in one town claimed he had sold a wheat crop illegally, and government inspectors found some irregular entries in his account books. It turned out that his assistant was at fault, and so Cervantes was not prosecuted.

However, his honesty had been questioned. This not only hurt his feelings, but it also damaged his reputation. The importance Cervantes placed on maintaining his honor can be seen in a line he wrote later in his most famous novel: "[I]f I take away your honor it is plain I take away your life, as a man without honor is worse than dead."

Cervantes could not then foresee that his honor would be soon questioned again—this time with serious consequences. ✑

In *May 1590,*
Cervantes' sister
Magdalena sent a
letter to King Philip
requesting that her
brother be given a job
in Spain's colonies in
the Caribbean. The
letter said in part:
"Miguel de Cervantes
… has served Your
Majesty many years
in the campaigns on
sea and land which
have occurred in the
past twenty-two years.
… He requests …
that Your Majesty be
pleased to favor him
with a post in the
Indies … because he is
an able and competent
man and deserving of
Your Majesty's favor."

Chapter
7 IN PRISON AGAIN

◦◦◦◦◦

By 1594, King Philip had given up on the idea of invading England again. He no longer needed contractors to raise large quantities of supplies for a giant fleet. As a result, Miguel de Cervantes suddenly found himself out of a job and unable to support his family. His mother had died the previous year, but he still had his wife and sisters to worry about.

Cervantes immediately requested that the government find other work for him. Various relatives also made pleas to the royal court on his behalf. They pointed out his distinguished military service at Lepanto and elsewhere. Surely, they thought, the government could find some kind of employment for a veteran of his courage and stature.

Fortunately for Cervantes, someone in the

Sixteenth-century Dutch artist Marinus van Reymerswaele painted two tax collectors at work.

government heard these pleas. During his days as a contractor, he had developed a friendship with a government bookkeeper, Augustin de Cetina. Cetina now recommended him for a job as a royal tax collector. In August 1594, Cervantes accepted the position. He was assigned to the region of Granada,

An antique print of people in Granada during Cervantes' time

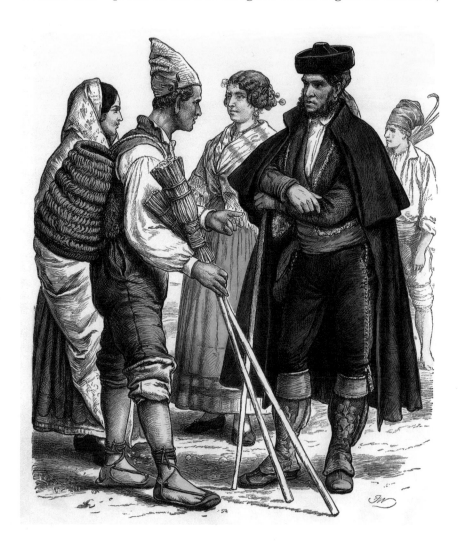

in southeastern Spain. His task was to collect back taxes owed by various towns in the area.

The position came with certain built-in drawbacks and advantages. One drawback, as Cervantes well knew, was that no one likes to pay taxes, and nearly everyone hates tax collectors. It was bound to be a stressful job. Another problem was that Cervantes would be handling large amounts of money. His personal credit history was not good. He had often been heavily in debt, and his honesty had been questioned while he was a contractor. For these reasons, the government now required him to provide certain financial guarantees. Among these, he had to list all his personal belongings. If any shortfalls appeared in his tax collection accounts, the government could legally seize these possessions.

Among the advantages of the job was good pay. His daily wages were to be twice as much as he had made as a contractor. The government also gave him broad powers to help enforce his collection demands. If a town official refused to pay, for example, he could sue or even imprison the official. He could also seize and auction off people's possessions.

Cervantes produced no important literary works in the mid-1590s. However, it appears that he still wrote some poetry when he could find the time. Early in 1595, he entered a poetry-writing contest sponsored by the Dominican monks in the town of Saragossa. He won the contest, earning a prize of three silver spoons.

*The 1563
Civitates Orbis
Terrarum by
Georg Braun
and Frans
Hogenberg
depicts
Granada.*

Using these powers—or the threat of them—
Cervantes successfully collected most of the back
taxes in the Granada region. He sent most of the
money directly to the national treasury in Madrid.
Of the many towns that owed money, only three did
not pay in full. But in one of the three, Véléz-Málaga,
Cervantes managed to collect almost half of the
amount owed. Before returning to Madrid with the
money, he stopped off in Seville. It had struck him
that it might not be wise to carry so much cash on
his person. After all, what if he was robbed? So he

deposited the money in a local bank run by Simon Freire de Lima. The bank gave him a receipt he could use later to collect the funds at a bank in Madrid.

Cervantes was unaware at the time that forces he could not control would soon drive him to the brink of ruin. When he arrived in Madrid, he tried to withdraw the money. To his surprise and horror, he was told that Lima had just declared bankruptcy. Even worse, the banker had stolen some of the funds from his bank and fled. Cervantes and others suspected that Lima had gone to the Americas. It was not difficult to arrange passage in one of the many galleys headed to the West Indies, a common refuge for Spaniards with money problems or criminal backgrounds.

Unable to chase Lima across the Atlantic Ocean, the desperate Cervantes hurried to Seville. Lima's house and other property were worth a considerable amount. By legal means, Cervantes was able to recover the lost money from the man's estate. He deposited the funds in the national treasury in January 1597, but the damage had already been done. He had lost his

> *The Spanish West Indies were just a small part of the larger Spanish presence in the Americas. After Christopher Columbus' expedition in 1492, Spain began gobbling up land in the New World. By the end of the 16th century, Spain controlled Mexico, Central America, nearly all the West Indies, part of what is now the southwestern United States, and much of western South America.*

job. Moreover, the government refused to pay him most of the salary he had earned as a tax collector.

As if these blows to Cervantes' life and reputation were not enough, an even worse calamity struck in the summer of 1597. Treasury officials suddenly accused him of fraud. Government accountants claimed that large amounts of money he had collected in Granada had never made it into the treasury. It is now clear that the accountants were in error. Cervantes had made all the deposits, and no money was missing. At the time, however, the case against him looked convincing. A Seville judge ordered that he be thrown into prison.

Cervantes' cell in the Seville jail is now part of the Museum Casa de Medrano.

For the second time in his life, Cervantes found himself behind bars with no idea when he would be released. In Algiers, the Turks had been ready to hold him for as long as it took to collect a ransom. This time was little different. The judge did not specify the length of the sentence. Cervantes would remain confined either until he paid the debt he supposedly owed or until the government and court were satisfied.

But Cervantes did have two advantages over most of the other prisoners. First, he had experienced firsthand the awful conditions in a foreign prison. Nothing he witnessed in the Seville jail surprised or horrified him. Also, his quarters in the jail were better than those of most of his fellow inmates. Biographer Francisco Ledesma explains:

> Miguel was destined, not to be put in irons or assigned to the galleries, prison areas where dangerous prisoners were confined … but to the upper halls next to the infirmary and near the warden's quarters. Miguel's crime was considered a misfortune or

Cervantes witnessed numerous colorful and dramatic characters and events while he was in the Seville jail. Among the more emotional moments were those in which condemned men went to their deaths. A prisoner who was about to die shook hands with the other prisoners in his section. Then, when the guards came to take him away, the inmates cursed and threw human waste at them. Afterwards, the prisoners lit candles and sang a hymn for the dead man.

Cervantes used his time in prison to work on a new book.

misadventure rather than a crime as such, and it would not be fit for a prisoner of such minor importance to be confused with the mass of killers, ruffians, [and] swindlers.

Still, even for someone in Cervantes' position, the conditions in the prison were miserable. There was a constant high level of noise as inmates complained, argued, fought, cursed, and prayed. Some men smuggled weapons inside. Others bribed the guards to let them have visits by women or to spend the time outside the jail. And still others stole items from visitors and auctioned them off to use as bribes. Nothing was done to stop of any of this, Cervantes noted, because the corrupt warden received a cut of all the action.

While in prison in Algiers, Cervantes had shown himself to be a resourceful, creative individual. Most of that creativity had gone into his many escape attempts. In the Seville jail, by contrast, Cervantes channeled his creativity in a different way. Shutting out much of the chaos and the nastiness around him, he began imagining the plot and characters of a new novel. A man down on his luck and penniless was about to produce something priceless—a book for the ages. ❧

8 CREATING A MASTERPIECE

Chapter

❧❧❧

While he was in the Seville jail, Miguel de Cervantes wisely used his writing skills to try to gain his freedom. In a letter to the king, he explained that he had been wrongly convicted. He also implored King Philip to order his release from the prison. The king did so. Cervantes most likely left the jail in early December 1597, although some evidence suggests that there may have been legal complications that kept Cervantes locked up until April 1598.

Almost nothing is known about Cervantes' whereabouts and activities in the six years following his release. Apparently he did not have a steady job. He and his wife must have been poverty-stricken—or nearly so. Still, the couple traveled a lot, spending time in Madrid, nearby Toledo, and the

Don Quixote and Sancho Panza rode off to battle evil in a 19th-century painting by Alexandre Gabriel Decamps.

village of Esquivias.

What seems certain is that Cervantes spent much of his time in these years writing his great novel *Don Quixote*. A true masterpiece of fiction, it is a fantasy that mixes elements of humor and drama. On one level, the novel is a satire, or spoof, of romances. These were adventure tales that were widely popular in Spain and other parts of Europe in late medieval times. A typical romance featured a brave knight who battled evil and performed heroic, often superhuman feats. Most of these tales were unoriginal and poorly written, and Cervantes felt that people read too many of them and took them too seriously.

To poke fun at the romances, Cervantes had his main character be obsessed with reading them. That character is a Spanish landowner named Alonso Quixano, in his 50s. Years of reading too much and sleeping too little have caused him to go mad. He has come to believe that he is one of the heroes from the romances, a knight named Don Quixote de La Mancha. Cervantes sums up the basic premise of the novel in the opening of the first chapter:

> *In short, his wits being quite gone, he hit upon the strangest notion that ever a madman in this world hit upon, and that was that he fancied it was right ... that he should make a knight-errant of himself, roaming the world over in full armor and*

on horseback in quest of adventures, ... righting every kind of wrong, and exposing himself to peril and danger from which ... he was to reap eternal renown and fame. ... [A]nd so, led away by the intense enjoyment he found in these pleasant fancies, he set himself forthwith to put his scheme into execution.

In a 1920 painting, Don Quixote sat in his study reading old stories about brave knights.

Quixote is accompanied in his adventures by a neighbor, Sancho Panza, who leaves his farm work to serve as the mad knight's squire, or assistant. During their journeys together, Quixote continually mistakes ordinary people and things for bigger or better ones. For instance, he sees a small, shoddy inn

In the novel, other characters can see that Don Quixote is not really a heroic knight. In Part Two, a man approaches him and tries to get him to face reality. The man says: "You are mad; and if you were so by yourself, ... it would not be so bad; but you have the gift of making fools and blockheads of all who have anything to do with you or say to you. Why, look at these gentlemen bearing you company! Get you home, blockhead, ... and give [up] these fooleries that are sapping your brains and skimming away your wits."

as a lofty castle, and he is convinced that a lowly peasant girl is a noble lady whose honor he must protect. Quixote also launches a full-scale attack on some windmills, which he thinks are bloodthirsty giants.

Cervantes completed what turned out to be Part One of *Don Quixote* sometime in 1604. His search for a publisher took him to Francisco de Robles, in Madrid. Robles' father, Blas de Robles, had published Cervantes' first novel, *La Galatea*, many years before. The son immediately saw the new novel as a work of genius and agreed to publish it. The first edition appeared in March 1605.

Don Quixote was an enormous hit with the reading public. The first edition of the book quickly sold out, breaking all previous publishing records. More editions followed. Soon the novel was translated into French, German, Italian, and English.

Cervantes had become a famous and respected writer at last. However, the book did not bring him riches, which he had hoped it would. All he received for the work was a single fee, for which he gave all

the rights to the novel to Robles. As Cervantes was well aware, such unfair treatment of writers was then commonplace, but an author basically had no other

Believing it to be a giant, Don Quixote charged at a windmill— with disastrous results.

81

EL INGENIOSO
HIDALGO DON QVI.
xote de la Manoha.

Compuesto por Miguel de Ceruantes Saauedra.

DIRIGIDO AL DVOVE DE
Bejar. Marques de Gibraleon,. Conde de Benalcacar,
Bañares, Vizconde dela Poebla de Alcozer. Señor
de las villas de Capilla, Curiel,
y Burguillos.

Impreffo con licencia, en Valençia, en cafa de
Pedro Patricio Mey, 1605.

A cofta de Iufepe Ferrer mercader de libros,
delante la Dipucacion;

choice. The only alternative was for him to publish the book at his own expense, and that was too big a risk, since the finished product might not sell well.

Cervantes expressed how he felt about these matters in a scene in *Don Quixote* in which the mad knight converses with an author who has just written a book. The man says he is going to publish the book himself, at his own expense. Quixote tells him:

> [I]t is plain you don't know the ins and outs of the printers, and how they play into one another's hands. I promise you when you find yourself saddled with two thousand copies you will feel so sore that it will astonish you, particularly if the book is a little out of the common and not in any way highly spiced.

Partly to cash in on the popularity of *Don Quixote*, Cervantes eventually began work on a sequel. He was finishing the 59th chapter in the fall of 1614 when distressing news arrived. Another writer had just published his own sequel to Cervantes' novel. No copyright laws existed at the time, so one author could legally get away with stealing another's ideas.

There was only one thing Cervantes could do to protect his literary property. He had to finish Part Two of *Don Quixote* and publish it as quickly as possible. This he managed to do in the space of only a few months. The sequel was released to the public in November 1615. It was hugely successful and rapidly pushed the other version into obscurity.

Don Quixote sat in his study surrounded by characters from his adventures in a 19th-century engraving.

Cervantes wanted to make sure that copycat writers could not write any more bogus sequels to *Don Quixote*, so he had his main character die in the end of Part Two. After Quixote's demise, the author warns others:

> [L]eave at rest where they lie the weary moldering bones of Don Quixote, and not to attempt to carry him off, ... making him rise from the grave where in reality and truth he lies stretched at full length, powerless to make any third expedition.

Cervantes himself reserved the right, of course, to find a way of bringing Quixote back. However, this was a path the writer was not destined to take. He had no way of knowing it, but only a few months after the release of Part Two he would be dead. ℭ

9 LAST YEARS AND LEGACY

❧⟨✕⟩❧

Miguel de Cervantes' final decade of life was, professionally speaking, busy and productive. After the success of Part One of *Don Quixote*, he spent most of his time writing. Everything he turned out was eventually published. However, his personal life proved less successful. He never made much money from his writing, and he remained nearly always on the verge of poverty. Also, almost everyone close to him either died or walked out on him.

There was no way that Cervantes could have foreseen this unhappy scenario. In fact, in 1604, when he was finishing Part One of *Don Quixote*, he was literally surrounded by family. He was apparently as happy as he had ever been. That year, he moved from Esquivias to Valladolid. There he rented a second-story apartment that overlooked a charming river scene. Living with him in the apartment were his wife, Doña Catalina, his sisters, Andrea and Magdalena, and his niece, Constanza.

Also living in the apartment was Cervantes' daughter, Isabel. Somewhat earlier, her mother had died and the young woman had discovered that Cervantes was her birth father. The details of their reunion are unknown, but it seems that he insisted on supporting her. Doña Catalina reluctantly accepted her into the family.

In 1606, not long after Part One of *Don Quixote* was published, Cervantes, now 59, moved the family again. This time he settled in Madrid. At the time, he was already writing a series of short stories. Each commented on some social or political issue then current in Spain. There were 11 stories in all, with titles such as "The Little Gypsy Girl," "The Lady Cornelia," "The Force of Blood," and "The Deceitful Marriage." Cervantes collected the stories and eventually published them under the title *Exemplary Novels*.

While in Madrid, Cervantes worked on other

Cervantes' only child, Isabel, had a difficult life as a young adult. In 1606, not long after moving in with her father, she got married and had a child. The little girl was named Isabel, after her mother. Two years later, the husband died. Three months after that, the elder Isabel married again. In 1610, the younger Isabel died, leaving her mother grief-stricken.

Cervantes spent his last years in a comfortable house in Madrid, Spain.

writing projects as well. One was a much longer story—a novel titled *The Trials of Persiles and Sigismunda*. A sort of fairy tale, it describes two young people in love. They have a series of adventures and eventually get married in Rome. Also in these years, Cervantes wrote a long poem, "The Journey to Parnassus." A witty fantasy, it tells how some good and bad poets go to Greece, where they battle for literary supremacy.

The problem with these and other works Cervantes produced was that they earned him very little money. The quality of his writing was always high. However, he worked at a slow and deliberate pace. He also tended to work on several pieces at the same time. For these reasons, *Exemplary Novels* was not published until 1613, and "The Journey to Parnassus" did not reach the public until a year later.

While he was working on these pieces, Cervantes experienced financial difficulties. For a while, his sisters helped to pay the rent. But then both sisters moved out and became nuns. Both died of illness soon afterward. For reasons that are now unclear, Cervantes' wife, Doña Catalina, also joined a convent. And not long after that, a dispute over money motivated Isabel to cut all ties with her father.

Alone, in the spring of 1616 Cervantes became ill. It was soon clear that he was dying. The cause is uncertain, but modern experts theorize that he had diabetes, a disease then unknown to doctors. At the time, *The Trials of Persiles and Sigismunda* was finished but not yet published. On April 20, he added a prologue to the novel, which reads in part:

> *My life is coming to an end and by the calendar of my pulse, which at the latest will complete its course this Sunday, I will end that of my life. ... A time will perhaps*

come when I can pick up the broken thread and say what I have failed to say here and what I know I should be saying. Farewell to graceful speeches, farewell to witty sayings, farewell to fun-loving friends. I am dying and longing to see you soon making merry in the other world.

A March 26, 1616, letter to the archbishop of Toledo shows Cervantes' handwriting.

As he had predicted he would, Cervantes died three days later, on April 23, 1616. He was 68. The burial took place in the Trinitarian monastery located a few blocks from his home in Madrid. The monks erected no cross or stone to mark his gravesite.

In September, Doña Catalina made a deal that

allowed a bookseller, Juan de Villarroel, to publish *The Trials of Persiles and Sigismunda*. The book was released the following year. When she died in 1626, Villarroel still owed her money from its brisk sales.

Though popular in its day, *The Trials of Persiles and Sigismunda* became little more than a footnote in Cervantes' biography and cultural legacy. That enormous legacy rests mainly on his masterpiece, *Don Quixote*. Later generations of readers and literary critics came to see it as one of the greatest novels ever written. To date, it has gone through more than 700 editions. It has also been translated into every existing modern language.

In addition to its wide popularity as entertaining fiction, Cervantes' *Don Quixote* strongly influenced hundreds of later novelists. Among them were greats such as Charles Dickens, Jane Austen, James Joyce, and Gustave Flaubert. They saw in the mad knight's purity and courage what 19th-century Russian

Though he wrote poems, plays, and stories, Cervantes is primarily known for one novel—Don Quixote.

novelist Ivan Turgenev did. Turgenev wrote, "Don Quixote personifies above all the problem of faith, of faith in something eternal, … of faith in a truth higher than the individual." That truth, Turgenev pointed out, is the triumph of goodness and justice over evil and injustice.

These and other qualities made Don Quixote appealing to a wide range of artists over the centuries. Painters such as Pablo Picasso and Salvador Dali created now-famous images of the adventures of the mad knight and his squire. Composers captured

Spanish artist Pablo Picasso created a famous drawing of Don Quixote and Sancho Panza in 1955.

the spirit of those same adventures in their music. Several operas and ballets were based on Cervantes' novel. Also, German composer Richard Strauss wrote a long, single-movement piece titled *Don Quixote: Fantastic Variations on a Theme of Knightly Character*. The cello is used to represent Don Quixote, and the viola represents Sancho Panza. In one section, Strauss uses a wind machine to depict Quixote and Panza riding through the air. Perhaps the most famous musical piece based on the novel is the colorful Broadway show *Man of La Mancha*, which opened in New York City in 1965.

The tremendous influence of *Don Quixote* and the thousands of creative works based on it have made it an eternal part of world culture. But this great work should not be viewed separately from the man who created it. The fictional Don Quixote is in many ways very much like the real Miguel de Cervantes. Like his mad knight, Cervantes was an idealist. Through his writing, he made his own beauty in a world filled with ugliness.

A "play within a play," Man of La Mancha begins in a prison where Miguel de Cervantes is awaiting trial. He tells the other inmates the story of Don Quixote. As he does, he becomes that character, and the inmates become the other characters in Quixote's story. The original production opened on Broadway in November 1965, and a movie version of the play was made in 1972.

Don Quixote and Sancho Panza ride forth to new adventures in the Plaza de España in Madrid.

Also like Quixote, Cervantes believed in fighting for what is right, even against seemingly impossible odds. Despite many misfortunes, including poverty and years spent in prison, Cervantes never gave up. He rose to the challenge and created great literature for the ages. He recognized that he and Quixote were inseparable, writing in the book's conclusion: "For me alone was Don Quixote born, and I for him; it was his to act, mine to write; we two together make but one." ℬ

CERVANTES' LIFE

1547

Born on or about September 29 in Alcalá de Henares, Spain

1555

May have attended a Jesuit school in Córdoba

1564

Moves with his family to Seville, in southern Spain

1545

1545

The Catholic Counter-Reformation begins in Europe

1555

Artist Michelangelo destroys his Florentine *Pietà* sculpture, which was to be used on his tomb; it is later repaired and is on display in Florence, Italy

1564

Poet and playwright William Shakespeare is born

WORLD EVENTS

1568

Writes some poems to mark the untimely death of the Spanish queen

1569

Travels to Rome and begins working at the Vatican

1571

Fights the Turks in the naval battle of Lepanto, in Greece

1570

1566

St. Augustine, in present-day Florida, is founded by the Spanish

1570

The potato is introduced to Europe from South America

CERVANTES' LIFE

1575

Captured at sea and
confined in a Turkish
prison in North Africa

1576

Stages the first
of several escape
attempts

1580

Gains release
from prison

1575

1577

Francis Drake sails
around the world by
way of Cape Horn

1576

English navigator Martin Frobisher,
on his search for the Northwest
Passage, enters the Canadian bay
that now bears his name

WORLD EVENTS

1585

Publishes his first
novel, *La Galatea*

1587

Begins working as a
government supply
contractor

1584

Marries Doña
Catalina de Salazar

1585

1589

Galileo Galilei
becomes professor of
mathematics at the
University of Pisa

1582

Pope Gregory XIII
invents a calendar that
more closely follows
the seasonal year than
the Julian calendar
then in use

1587

Virginia Dare is born on
Roanoke Island off the coast
of North Carolina to become
the first child born of English
parents in North America

CERVANTES' LIFE

1605

Publishes Part One
of his masterpiece,
Don Quixote

1597

Imprisoned in
Seville on charges
of misplacing tax
monies

1594

Begins working
as a government
tax collector

1600

1603

James I becomes
king of England
and Ireland

1597

The world's first
opera is performed
in Florence, Italy

WORLD EVENTS

1615

Publishes Part Two
of *Don Quixote*

1613

Publishes
Exemplary Novels,
a collection of
short stories

1616

Dies April 23 in
Madrid, probably of
diabetes

1615

1620

The *Mayflower*
with its Pilgrim
passengers sails
from England to
North America

1611

The King James
Bible, commissioned
by the British king,
is published

DATE OF BIRTH: On or about
September 29, 1547

BIRTHPLACE: Alcalá de Henares, Spain

FATHER: Don Rodrigo de
Cervantes (c. 1509–1585)

MOTHER: Doña Leonor de Cortinas
(c. 1520–1593)

SPOUSE: Doña Catalina de Salazar
(1565–1626)

DATE OF MARRIAGE: December 12, 1584

CHILDREN: Isabel de Saavedra
(c. 1585–1652; with
Ana Franca de Rojas)

DATE OF DEATH: April 23, 1616

PLACE OF BURIAL: Trinitarian monastery,
Madrid, Spain

FURTHER READING

Andrade, Marcel Charles, ed. *Classic Spanish Stories and Plays: The Great Works of Spanish Literature for Intermediate Students.* Chicago: McGraw-Hill, 2001.

Bicheno, Hugh. *Crescent and Cross: The Battle of Lepanto, 1571.* London: Phoenix, 2004.

Bloom, Harold, ed. *Miguel de Cervantes.* Philadelphia: Chelsea House Publishers, 2005.

Parker, Barbara Keevil, and Duane F. Parker. *Miguel de Cervantes.* Philadelphia: Chelsea House Publishers, 2003.

Patterson, Benton Rain. *With the Heart of a King: Elizabeth I of England, Philip II of Spain, and the Fight for a Nation's Soul and Crown.* New York: St. Martin's Press, 2007.

Tincey, John. *The Spanish Armada.* Oxford: Osprey, 2000.

LOOK FOR MORE SIGNATURE LIVES
BOOKS ABOUT THIS ERA:

Christopher Columbus: *Explorer of the New World*

Elizabeth I: *Queen of Tudor England*

Johannes Gutenberg: *Inventor of the Printing Press*

Michelangelo: *Sculptor and Painter*

Francisco Pizarro: *Conqueror of the Incas*

William Shakespeare: *Playwright and Poet*

On the Web

For more information on this topic, use FactHound.

1. Go to *www.facthound.com*
2. Type in this book ID: 0756536758
3. Click on the *Fetch It* button.

FactHound will find the best Web sites for you.

Historic Sites

Cervantes Birthplace Museum
Mayor, 48
28801 Alcalá de Henares, Spain
91.889.96.54
Museum housed in the building where Cervantes was born

Village of Esquivias
Centro Urbano
Toledo, Spain
34.925.520161
Village where Cervantes and his wife were married and the house in which they lived